T0065701

CUTTING IT STRAIGHT

*The Key To Dynamic Expository Preaching
and Powerful Biblical Presentations*

JAMES A. BYRD

WESTBOW
PRESS®
A DIVISION OF THOMAS NELSON
& ZONDERVAN

Copyright © 2022 James A. Byrd.

All rights reserved. No part of this book may be used or reproduced by any means, graphic, electronic, or mechanical, including photocopying, recording, taping or by any information storage retrieval system without the written permission of the author except in the case of brief quotations embodied in critical articles and reviews.

This book is a work of non-fiction. Unless otherwise noted, the author and the publisher make no explicit guarantees as to the accuracy of the information contained in this book and in some cases, names of people and places have been altered to protect their privacy.

WestBow Press books may be ordered through booksellers or by contacting:

WestBow Press
A Division of Thomas Nelson & Zondervan
1663 Liberty Drive
Bloomington, IN 47403
www.westbowpress.com
844-714-3454

Because of the dynamic nature of the Internet, any web addresses or links contained in this book may have changed since publication and may no longer be valid. The views expressed in this work are solely those of the author and do not necessarily reflect the views of the publisher, and the publisher hereby disclaims any responsibility for them.

Any people depicted in stock imagery provided by Getty Images are models, and such images are being used for illustrative purposes only.
Certain stock imagery © Getty Images.

Scripture marked (KJV) taken from the King James Version of the Bible.

Scripture marked (NKJV) taken from the New King James Version®. Copyright © 1982 by Thomas Nelson. Used by permission. All rights reserved.

Scripture quotations marked (NIV) are taken from the Holy Bible, New International Version®, NIV®. Copyright © 1973, 1978, 1984, 2011 by Biblica, Inc.® Used by permission of Zondervan. All rights reserved worldwide. www. zondervan.com The "NIV" and "New International Version" are trademarks registered in the United States Patent and Trademark Office by Biblica, Inc.®

Scripture quotations marked (ESV) are from the ESV® Bible (The Holy Bible, English Standard Version®), copyright © 2001 by Crossway, a publishing ministry of Good News Publishers. Used by permission. All rights reserved. The ESV text may not be quoted in any publication made available to the public by a Creative Commons license. The ESV may not be translated into any other language.

Scripture quotations marked (NASB) taken from the (NASB®) New American Standard Bible®, Copyright © 1960, 1971, 1977, 1995, 2020 by The Lockman Foundation. Used by permission. All rights reserved. www.lockman.org

ISBN: 978-1-6642-8207-0 (sc)
ISBN: 978-1-6642-8208-7 (hc)
ISBN: 978-1-6642-8206-3 (e)

Library of Congress Control Number: 2022919599

Print information available on the last page.

WestBow Press rev. date: 10/21/2022

ACKNOWLEDGMENTS

Paul writes in 1 Corinthians 15:1(KVJ) "But by the grace of God I am what I am: and his grace which was bestowed upon me was not in vain; but I laboured more abundantly than they all: yet not I, but the grace of God which was with me." *54*

I thank God the Father of my Lord and Savior Jesus Christ and the sanctifying Holy Spirit who convicted me when I heard the glorious gospel of God that saved me through faith in Christ when I believed and obeyed. I also thank all the men and women who allowed God's grace to work thorough them on my behalf.

I thank my dearest wife Leatta, who has been with me through all my trials, listened to all my dreams, and supported all my endeavors. I must not forget to thank Betty, a Godsend who proofed and typed my manuscript.

I hope and pray that the readers of this guide will consider my humble attempt to share my Biblically based thoughts. The intent of this guide is to encourage the herald of God's Word to speak as

His oracle, forsake all human inventions of the mind, and speak the Word of God in sincerity and truth.

May God find favor with all of us so that our preaching will call men and women out of the darkness of despair into the marvelous light of salvation.

Dr. James A. Byrd

TABLE OF CONTENTS

Part III: Interpreting the Message

Part IV: Developing the Message

Part V: Delivering the Sermon/Biblical Presentation

Part VI: Good News You Can Use

Be diligent to present yourself approved to God, a worker who does not need to be ashamed, rightly dividing the word of truth.

—2 TIMOTHY 2:15 (NKJV)

INTRODUCTION

Be diligent to present yourself approved to God, a
worker who does not need to be ashamed, *rightly
dividing the word of truth* [emphasis added]. But shun
profane and idle babblings, for they will increase to
more ungodliness. And their message will spread like
cancer. Hymenaeus and Philetus are of this sort, who have
strayed concerning the truth, saying that the resurrection
is already past; and they overthrow the faith of some.

—2 TIMOTHY 2:15–18 (NKJV)

Paul is writing to the young preacher Timothy, encouraging him
to be a diligent worker for God, rightly dividing the word of truth.
"Rightly dividing" comes from the Greek word *orthotomounta,* which
literally means "cutting straight." Some expositors suggest that this
word is a metaphor that describes plowing a straight furrow, while
others argue that the word symbolizes a stonemason cutting stones
straight. I believe now is the time for those who preach the Good
News of the kingdom of God to begin cutting it straight. This means

rightly dividing the word of truth by preaching the "whole counsel of God" (Acts 20:27 NKJV) that requires expository preaching from the Old Testament canon that is uniquely Christian.

The questions that beg to be answered are: What is expository preaching? Why is expository preaching from the Old Testament needed?

What is expository preaching? John MacArthur, Jr., in his book *Rediscovering Expository Preaching*, sums up expository preaching in three keywords: inductive, exegetical, and expositional. Expository preaching is inductive in that we approach the text without any preconceived attitudes or ideas about the text under consideration. Expository preaching is exegetical because the expositor must use a sound hermeneutical process to determine the original meaning of the text (1992, page number). In *Expository Preaching: The Art of Preaching Through the Bible*, Harold T. Bryson posits that the exegete performs the role of historian, grammarian, literary analyst, philologist, and theologian to discover the original meaning of the text (1995, page number).

Expository preaching is expositional and is accomplished by using proper homiletics to transport the original meaning of the text to the hearers of today. The Bible gives us an eternal definition of exposition in Nehemiah 8:8 (NIV): "They read from the book, from the Law of God clearly, and give the sense so that the people understood the reading."

Expository preaching grounds the message in the Word of God. God's Word will accomplish God's purpose for our lives. The gospel prophet Isaiah writes, "So shall my word be that which goes out from my mouth, it shall not return to me empty but it shall accomplish that which I purpose and shall succeed in the thing which I sent it" (Isaiah 55:11 KJV).

If preachers desire to accomplish that which God proposes, we must perform expository preaching from the Old Testament as well as the New Testament. We must "rightly [divide] the word of truth." We must perform our duties as one who cuts it straight.

I sincerely hope this manual will inspire contemporary preacher, as well myself, to present the whole counsel of God from Genesis through Revelation.

We know what expository preaching is, but why should we perform expository preaching from the Old Testament?

For whatsoever things were written aforetime were written for our learning, that we through patience and comfort of the scriptures might have hope.

ROMANS 15:4 (KVJ)

Chapter 1

THE WHAT AND WHY OF EXPOSITORY PREACHING FROM THE OLD TESTAMENT

For whatsoever things were written aforetime were
written for our learning, that we through patience
and comfort of the scriptures might have hope.

—ROMANS 15:4 (KJV)

There are at least four reasons to practice expository preaching from the Old Testament: to gain wisdom and equipment for every good work; to set the background for the understanding of the New Testament; to point to Christ for the learning of patience, comfort, and hope; and to prevent repeating the Marcion heresy.

In order for God's people to become wise to their salvation, the Old Testament must be proclaimed. In 2 Timothy 3:10–14 (KJV), Paul charges Timothy to "continue in what you have learned and became convinced of, because you know those from whom you have learned it, and how from infancy you have known the holy Scriptures which are able to make you wise for salvation through faith in Christ Jesus." Note that the Holy Scriptures at the time 2 Timothy was written refer to the Old Testament in Christ Jesus. By this, I mean that the Old Testament can give us sufficient faith to point us to Christ, where we will find our salvation.

In 2 Timothy 3:16–17 (KJV), we note that "all Scripture Testament. Therefore, we may conclude that the Old Testament makes one wise for salvation through faith is God breathed" (v. 16), and it is "God's way of preparing us in every way fully equipped for every good thing God wants us to do" (v. 17).

We must preach the Old Testament scriptures because the Old Testament is the background for understanding the New Testament. We cannot understand the New Testament without understanding the Old Testament because the New Testament is the completion of the Old Testament. Note that the New Testament is the fulfillment of all the Old Testament prophecies that testify of Christ Jesus. In John 5:39 (NKJV), the apostle quotes Jesus as saying, "'You diligently study the Scriptures because you think by them you have eternal life. These are the Scriptures which testify of me, yet you refuse to come to me.'"

The Old Testament scriptures spoke about Jesus Christ. They pointed to Christ. If we fail to preach the Old Testament, then it is easier for our people to be tricked by false teachers and liberal theologians who claim that the teachings of Jesus Christ in the gospels is a collection of mythological allegories. If Christ is a mythological character created by the church to jump-start Christianity, then what hope do we have? As the apostle Paul wrote in 1 Corinthians 15:1 (KJV), "And if Christ has not been raised, our preaching is useless and so is your faith." If we fail to preach Christ from the Old Testament, then the faith of the community can be overthrown by the false teachers of the twenty-first century.

We must proclaim the Old Testament scriptures for the community of faith's learning, their patience, their comfort, and their hope. We know that the Old Testament was not written primarily for the Old Testament saints, but as scripture testifies, it was written for the church of Christ. In Romans 15, the apostle Paul writes, "For everything that was written in the past was written to teach us [the body of Christ] so that through endurance and the encouragement of the Scriptures we might have hope." Some commentators posit that the hope of Christians is the surety of the Lord. Hope is perfect assurance or absolute confidence in the glory of God.

In Romans 8:5–39 (KJV), Paul asks this question in verse 35:

> Who shall separate us from the love of Christ? Shall
> trouble or hardship or persecution or famine or

nakedness or sword? As it is written, for your sakes we face death all day long; we are considered as sheep for the slaughter. No, in all these things we are more than conquerors through him who loved us.

Here, Paul uses Isaiah 44:22 (KJV) as an example of life circumstances in which believers found themselves during Old Testament times, Although certain martyrdom (the sword) may have been in their future, nothing should move them from the surety (hope) of the love of God that is found only in Christ. Paul encourages and builds up hope in the Roman believers in spite of almost unlivable circumstances. God always loves us in spite of our circumstances. We must proclaim the Old Testament scriptures so that our people may understand the surety of their hope for glory.

We must proclaim the Old Testament to prevent duplication of the Marcion heresy. As Elizabeth Achtemeier writes, "If we ignore the first two thirds of the Bible from the pulpit, we preach a truncated gospel" (1989, page number). By ignoring the Old Testament, we do not allow our people to become "wise unto their salvation though Christ Jesus" (2 Timothy 3:14 KJV). Achtemeier also suggests that the "failure to preach the Old Testament canon leaves people with no means for properly understanding and appropriating the Christian faith" (1989, page number).

If people are to become "wise unto their salvation through Christ Jesus," the expository preaching from the Old Testament canon must be uniquely Christian. This manual will guide you through principles that are useful in the Old Testament as well as the New Testament. Let's get started by cutting it straight!

PART I

PREPARING THE MESSENGER

For our gospel came not unto you in word only,
but also in power, and in the Holy Ghost, and
in much assurance; as ye know what manner of
men we were among you for your sake.

—1 THESSALONIANS 1:5 (KJV)

Chapter 2

CUTTING IT STRAIGHT BY PLUGGING INTO THE POWER SOURCE

> For our gospel came not unto you in word only,
> but also in power, and in the Holy Ghost, and
> in much assurance; as ye know what manner of
> men we were among you for your sake.
>
> **—1 THESSALONIANS 1:5 (KJV)**

*I*f a preacher desires to give the Lord's people a word from the Lord, he or she must be plugged into the power of God. The preacher does this by proper spiritual preparation that consists of at least three elements: prayer, piety, and passion.

Prayer is the foundation on which biblical sermons are built. Paul writes in 1 Corinthians 2:1, 12 (NIV),

> For who among men knows the thoughts of a man
> except the man's spirit within him? In the same way

no one knows the thoughts of God except the Spirit of God…We have not received the spirit of the world but the Spirit who is from God, that we may understand what God has freely given us.

The preacher is at the mercy of God to give the people of God the word of grace to minister to their needs. The minister does not know the hearts of those to whom he or she must speak, and the minister doesn't know the mind of God or the thoughts of God. Isaiah writes in Isaiah 55:8–9 (ESV), "For my thoughts are not your thoughts and neither are my ways your ways, declares the Lord, for as the heavens are higher than the earth, so are my ways higher then your ways and my thoughts your thoughts."

If the expositor wants to preach a biblical sermon, he or she must plug in to the power source through prayer and wait for an answer. In Jeremiah 42:2–3 (NIV), a prophet of God writes that military leaders approached

> Jeremiah the prophet and said to him, "Please hear our petition and pray to the Lord your God for this entire remnant. For as you now see, though we were once many, now only a few are left. Pray that the Lord your God will tell us where we should go and what we should do."

Let the preacher be "instant in prayer" so that the people of God may have a faith that rests on the power of God and not in the wisdom of humans.

The preacher not only must be instant in prayer but he or she must also walk the talk. By this, I am suggesting that he or she must be an example to the believers. Bryan Chapell, in his book, *Christ-Centered Preaching,* suggests that "good preaching in one sense involves getting out of the way so the Word can work" (1994, page number). As someone once said, "The preacher is such a rascal, I can't hear a word he is saying."

Based on the rhetorical distinctions formulated by Aristotle, Chapell further elucidates that "communication involves *logos* (logic), *pathos* (emotive), and *ethos* (perceived character of the speaker)" (1994, page number; emphasis added). Chapell suggests that logos, pathos, and ethos are features of the speaker by which the hearer evaluates the truth of what is being heard. Persuasive speech requires that none of those features become stumbling blocks to the message. Chapell also states that Aristotle believed "ethos to be the most powerful component of persuasion" (1994, page number).

The preacher must be aware that he or she must be an example to the believers.

In 1 Timothy 4:12 (NKJV), the apostle Paul writes, "Let no one despise your youth, but set believers an example in speech, in conduct, in love, in faith, in purity." In verse 16 of the same chapter,

Paul writes, "Keep a close watch on yourself and on your teaching, for by so doing, you will save both yourself and your hearers." Plugging in to the power not only involves prayer and piety but also a passion for preaching the Word of God. If we say we love the Lord Jesus Christ with a passionate love, then we must be lovers of the truth with the same passionate love, for Jesus Christ is *the way, the truth, and the life*" (John 14:6 NKJV; emphasis added). I believe that a passion for truth will encourage us to investigate the Word of God to the best of our ability as we seek to proclaim the "whole counsel of God" and not our own humanistic homilies. In 1 Peter 4:16 (NKJV), the apostle Peter writes, "If any man speaks, let him speak as an oracle of God." The apostle Paul writes in 1 Corinthians 2:4–5 (NKJV), "And my speech and my preaching was not with enticing words of man's wisdom, but in demonstration of the Spirit and of power That your faith should not stand in the wisdom of men, but in the power of God." I believe that is the ultimate test of our preaching. Now that we have plugged in to the power, let us select the preaching text anchoring the message in the Word of God.

All scripture is given by inspiration of God, and is profitable for doctrine, for reproof, for correction, for instruction in righteousness: That the man of God may be perfect, throughly furnished unto all good works.

—2 TIMOTHY 3:16-17 (KJV)

PART II

RESEARCHING
THE MESSAGE

Chapter 3

CUTTING IT STRAIGHT BY ANCHORING THE MESSAGE IN THE WORD OF GOD

All scripture is given by inspiration of God, and is profitable for doctrine, for reproof, for correction, for instruction in righteousness: That the man of God may be perfect, thoroughly furnished unto all good works.

—2 TIMOTHY 3:16–17 (KJV)

In order for the message to project the thoughts of God, it must be anchored in the word of God. If we want our people to have an "anchor for their souls," we must ground the message in the word of God. In order to perform sound biblical exposition, we must select a complete scriptural unit. This means that we must select one complete idea composed of multiple verses that support the one complete idea.

Bryson elucidates that the most frequent literary unit in a Bible book is its divisions into paragraphs. The down side of this is that the Bible has not always been divided into paragraphs, and the various translations have not been consistent in their paragraph designations. We shall consider a paragraph as a complete, unified thought. In other words, when the preacher selects a text for exposition, it should be a *complete unified thought or a thought unit.* Bryson suggests that a "paragraph consists of an assertion or thematic proposition with supporting propositions or may be a primary story with the reporting of supporting incidence, and it contains the framework for expressing and developing a single idea" (1995, page number).

There are three major types of paragraphs that one must understand in order to perform expository preaching from the Old Testament. Bryson identifies them as the narrative paragraph, the discourse paragraph, and the stanza or strophe. The narrative paragraph is a complete story with a common theme; the discourse paragraph is found primarily in the prophetic writings; and the stanza or strophe is used in the books of poetry (Bryson 1995, page number). This overview infers that we have in mind the *what* of selecting the text. Next, we will consider the basis of the text selection.

The scriptural unit or text is selected by two methods: by the lectionary or by personal preference. Each of these methods has its positives and negatives.

When one selects the text by the lectionary, most of the work of selecting an accurate text is done. This method is good from week to week, provides a balance for a preaching ministry, and helps a minister focus in on his or her favorite preaching topics. However, it is poor for addressing the perceived needs of the congregation. This method is a closed system and is not affected by the life situation of a particular congregation. One has to be careful when using the lectionary method as the selected text's delimiters may be affected by the theological bias of the author of the lectionary.

When we select the text by personal preference, we are able to address perceived needs of the congregation. The downside to the personal preference is that it lacks balance and can lead to hobby horsing (preaching your favorite subjects) or character assassination (singling out individuals in the congregation). Sidney Greidanus, in his book *The Modern Preacher and the Ancient Text: Interpreting And Preaching Biblical Literature*, suggests that "the danger of following one's predilection is that one may concentrate one's preaching on a narrow band of texts and fail to preach the whole counsel of God" (1988, page number). If we decide to use our personal preferences, then we will have to establish the boundaries of the selected text in order to insure we have a complete scriptural unit.

The boundaries of the selected text must be established to insure that we are not dealing with a fragment of a scriptural unit. The text must be a complete thought or scriptural unit that is sometimes referred to as a *pericope*. There are four types of analyses that I suggest the expositor use to establish the boundaries of the selected text if the preacher is not a Hebrew or Greek language scholar. They are contextual analysis, literary clues, rhetorical analysis, and conservative exegetical commentaries.

The preacher may use contextual analysis to examine the context immediately before and after the selected scriptural unit to determine that he or she has not detached the text from its intended place. Exegetical commentaries may be used to assist in establishing the delimiters of the selected scriptural unit.

Literary clues are also useful in determining the delimiters of the scriptural unit. Bryson suggests that the brief introduction of some Bible books designates the beginnings of a scriptural unit, such as in Jeremiah1:1–4 (KJV), in which the introduction establishes the beginning of the scriptural unit following verse four (1995, page number).

The major theme of the scriptural unit may also help determine the delimiters of the scriptural unit. Rhetorical analysis is an excellent tool to use for determining the theme of the scriptural unit. It provides an unbiased tool by forcing the preacher to leave his or her prejudices, presuppositions, and personal theology behind. The preacher is literally forced to find the delimiters of the scriptural unit inductively. Achtemeier provides an in-depth but understandable example of rhetorical analysis. Achtemeier shows that, through an analysis of key words, parallelisms, contrasts, changes in subject matter or speakers, and imperatives, one may determine the delimiters of the selected scriptural unit (1989, page number).

The preacher may also use conservative exegetical commentaries such as the *Pulpit Commentary, Keil Deletch*, or others to identify a complete scriptural unit. However, preachers should not be caught up in using commentaries to find the textual theme. A preacher may exegete the commentary instead of the text. Remember that *every commentator* has a personal theological bias or prejudice that may color his or her commentary. Once the preacher has a complete scriptural unit, he or she must then analyze the scriptural unit by "sharpening the sword."

> For the word of God is quick, and powerful, and sharper than any twoedged sword, piercing even to the dividing asunder of soul and spirit, and of the joints and marrow, and is a discerner of the thoughts and intents of the heart.
>
> **—HEBREWS 4:12 (KJV)**

Chapter 4

CUTTING IT STRAIGHT BY SHARPENING THE SWORD

For the word of God is quick, and powerful, and sharper
than any two-edged sword, piercing even to the dividing
asunder of soul and spirit, and of the joints and marrow,
and is a discerner of the thoughts and intents of the heart.

—HEBREWS 4:12 (KJV)

The preacher sharpens his or her sword with an in-depth study of
the scriptural unit to discover the meaning of the text when it was
written. The preacher must analyze the context of the scriptural
unit, the literary features of the scriptural unit, and the individual
sentences and words of the scriptural unit.

In his book *The Hermeneutical Spiral*, Grant R. Osborne suggests
that the first stage in serious Bible study is to consider the larger
context within which the passage is found. According to Osborne,

"Unless we can grasp the whole before attempting to dissect the parts, interpretation is doomed from the start" (1991, page number). Osborne suggests that the context is the historical context and the logical context.

The historical context refers to examination of the writer of the book, to whom the book is written, the chronology, and the purpose of the book. In the Old Testament, we know that Israel is the recipient of the writing, and we identify the historical context to ensure that we are cutting it straight. Sound exegetical commentaries may serve as a resource to obtain this critical information.

Osborne's discussion on the "logical context" provides excellent insight for understanding the effect of the context upon our interpretation. However, Bryson gives a more practical application for Old Testament expository preaching. Bryson writes that "the context refers to the connection of thought that runs through a passage that promotes the idea of a link that weaves the passage together in one piece" (1995, page number). If we violate the context, we *literally rip apart the thought.*

Therefore, we must examine the text in its book, section, immediate, and conical context. In Old Testament expository preaching, most of our focus will be on the book and the immediate and conical contexts. Since we will be performing thematic textual preaching (preaching from scriptural unit themes), we will not use the sectional context for our advantage. The contextual examination of the scriptural unit, both historically and logically (book, section, immediate, and conical), allows us to grasp the purpose and to frame the scriptural unit. We literally have the text interpreting us.

Next, we must look at the literary form that the original writer chose to convey God's message to the recipients. There are five types of Old Testament books that the preacher must proclaim. They are *narrative, law, prophetic, poetry,* and *wisdom.* The genre (literary type) of a Bible book will impact our interpretation. The genre of the book may provide clues to the rhetorical processes we will need as we move deeper into understanding the meaning of the text in terms of its original audience.

After the preacher has understood the genre of the book in which the scriptural unit is located, he or she should then identify the genre of the words of the text. All figures of speech should be known before we seek to discover the meaning of the words in the text. If a preacher confuses the literal and the figurative meaning of words in the selected text, he or she will naturally confuse his or her exegesis. Some of the basic figures of speech found in Biblical writings are metaphors, similes, hyperboles, and ironies. The preacher should be familiar with as many as possible.

A word study analysis of the text is done to discover the meaning of the words in the context that the author used them. Normally one would seek to do an etymological study of the key words in the passage. However, that type of study is not enough for proper exegesis of the passage. The etymological study gives the preacher information on the root or origin of a word but not its textual meaning.

Before we can interpret the text, we must discover the meaning of the words in the context of the passage. The words are studied in the selected passage to discover how they were used at the time the passage was written. As Bryson suggests, "The task of the exegete involves *discovering the meaning of the word, not determining its meaning*" (1995, page number; emphasis added). The preacher who is not proficient in the Hebrew or Greek languages may use concordances to study the various usages of words, and lexicons or Bible dictionaries to assist in determining the meaning of words in the text. No word study is complete without a syntactical study.

A syntactical study of the words of a passage is a study of how the "words, phrases, and clauses relate to each other." If the preacher is not proficient in the Hebrew language, he or she can use a literal English translation of the Bible as a basis for diagramming the passage. Diagramming the passage allows us to see how the parts of the text fit together. The preacher should familiarize himself or herself with at least six parts of speech: "subject, verb, object, adverb, adjective, and connectives, such as conjunctions, prepositions, and relative pronouns." By doing this, he or she will have the basic tools needed to diagram the passage. Multiple methods are needed in diagramming Old Testament passages because of the diverse genres of Bible books.

The *grammatical diagram,* or outline, shows the relationship of the words in a sentence and the subordinate clauses and phrases; this outline places the subject to far left, followed by the verb, and then the subject with the subordinate independent clauses and phrases beneath. If we apply this method to Psalms 1:1 (NIV), it appears as follows.

Psalm 1:1 (NIV) as it appears in the Biblical text

Blessed is the man

who does not walk in the counsel of the wicked

or stand in the way of sinners

or sit in the seat of mockers.

Grammatical outline of Psalm 1:1 (NIV)

The man who is blessed

does not walk in the counsel of the wicked

or stand in the way of sinners

or sit in the seat of mockers.

Another method for diagramming large portions of text covering many paragraphs is called the "conceptual" method. Chapell presents this method as an alternative, to be used with large portions of scripture. Chapell suggests that, in conceptual outlines, ideas, characters, and events that represent them (the sentences of the text) may be used instead of "precise phrases from the text" (1994, page number). "A statement listed in a conceptual outline may summarize several sentences. Below is the model using Dr. Richard Rogers outline from the Sunset International Bible Institute course *The Church in the Book of Acts.*

Outline Example for Longer Passages of Scripture

The Church Confirmed (Acts 3:1–4:37) (NIV)

A) The Miracle (Acts 3–11)

    1. Human Need)

        a) Extreme (1–2)

            1. The man lame and helpless
            2. The Place

    2. Divine Power (Acts 3:6–11)

B) Preaching (Acts 3:12–16)

    1. Self Preaching (v 12)
    2. God Honored (vs 13–14)
    3. Explanation Supplied (v 16)
    4. Exhortation Continued (vs 17–26)

C) The Persecution (Acts 4:1–3)

    1. Opposition Manifested (vs 1–4)

    2. Opposition Meet (vs 5–12)

    3. Opposition Matched (vs 13–18)

    4. Opposition Mastered (vs 19–22)

    5. Opposition Minimized

D) The Power (4:32–37)

    1. Collectively

        a) Reality Within (vs 32, 34, 35)

    2. Unity

    3. Unselfishness

        b) Prosperity Without (v 33)

    4. Individually (vs 36–37)

        a) The man (v 36)

        b) The money (v 37)

        c) The motive

These diagrams or outlines of a text will serve as exegetical outlines and may be used as bases for the sermon outline and corresponding flow of the sermon. We now have an idea of what themes are being presented in the scriptural unit, but the passage was not written in a vacuum. Since our goal is to perform expository preaching from the Old Testament that is uniquely Biblical and Christian, we must interpret the text in its own historical context. Therefore, we must rightly divide the *literary*, the *historical*, and the *theocentric* interpretations.

> But know this first of all, that no prophecy of
> Scripture is a matter of one's own interpretation.
>
> **—2 PETER 1:20 (NAS)**

PART III

INTERPRETING THE MESSAGE

Chapter 5

CUTTING IT STRAIGHT BY RIGHTLY DIVIDING THE INTERPRETATIONS

But know this first of all, that no prophecy of
Scripture is a matter of one's own interpretation.

—2 PETER 1:20 (NAS)

*B*y rightly dividing the interpretations, the preacher seeks to understand the selected text in the *literary setting*, the *historical setting*, and the *theological setting*.

When the preacher interprets the selected text with respect to these settings, he or she can avoid the atomization of the Biblical text that leads to a meaning other than what was intended by the original author. When the preacher rightly divides the interpretations, he or she seeks to *uncover the intended meaning* of the text that the inspired author had in mind.

Since we, as preachers, seek to preach the "whole counsel of God" (Acts 20:27; KJV), we must have a sound, repeatable method that allows us to account for all aspects that contribute to the author's intended meaning of the text. The interpretation of the selected text in its literary, historical, theological, and Christocentic aspects has been called the "holistic alternative" by Sidney Greidanus (1988, page number). However, we will interpret the text in the context of *three settings*: the *literary* setting, the *historical* setting, and the *theological* setting.

The literary setting consists of the literary forms and structures that the original author used to communicate his message. The literary aspect of interpretation seeks to discover how the text means and what the text means in the context of the book.

In answering the question "How does the text mean?" the preacher must determine the genre of the book, the genre of the text, and the genre of the figures of speech found within the text.

The major genres of the books in the Old Testament are the Hebrew narrative, law, prophetic, poetry, and wisdom. Knowing the genre of the Bible book helps the preacher determine the type of sermon form to use in developing the sermon. It also helps identify the mood of the book. For example, poetry communicates with emotion and figures of speech, while law is pragmatic and informative. The sermon form that the preacher uses should take into consideration the form that the original author used to effectively communicate the message. Disharmony between form and content of the sermon message may be disastrous. The genre of the book is paramount, but so is the genre of the text.

The genre of the text is extremely important for the preacher because of the diverse forms of literature within the prose passages of Old Testament books. There are legends, fables, contracts, autobiographies, and more. The preacher must know the form of literature with which he or she is working. In Exodus 15, we see the song of Miriam; the preacher must realize this fact in rightly dividing the Word of God. If one interprets a fable as a historical fact, the theological truth derived from the fable is in error. Not only should the preacher know the genre of the Bible book and the text, but he or she should also know the figures of speech within the text.

Some figures of speech found in the Old Testament are similes, personifications, and anthropomorphisms, to name a few. Figures of speech impact the interpretation of the text in a literal or figurative manner. W. Robert Palmer, writing in his book, *How to Interpret the Bible*, gives this example: "The Bible speaks of the 'hands,' 'back,' and 'face' of God" (1980, page number). This reference to Exodus 33:22 and 23 (KJV) does not mean that God literally has hands, a back, and a face.

The second question of our literary interpretation is "What did the text mean in the context of this Bible book?" We must understand what the major emphasis or the point of this text is in the context of the book. This question may be answered by examining the rhetorical structures of the text, such as repetitions, key words, literary parallelisms, inclusions, and chasms through the use of rhetorical analysis. Achtemeier provides an excellent in-depth example of rhetorical analysis in *Preaching from the Old Testament.*

The major genres of the Old Testament must be examined differently. The poetic and prophetical books may be analyzed by their parallelisms, repetitions of phrases, and repetition of key words to find the major point or theme of the passage. Homileticians suggest that we should pay attention to the parallelisms and whether they are synonymous, synthetic, or antithetic parallelisms. The ancient authors used parallelisms to express the same thought in a different way (synonymous), a series of thoughts leading to a climatic end (synthetic), or a contrast of thought (antithetic) to accentuate the point.

If the preacher is dealing with a historical narrative, he or she must examine the scenes, characters, and text from the characters' points of view, and the interactions between each character. Finally, the text must be viewed from God's point of view. The Holy Spirit is the narrator of the text, and God is the main attraction, as noted in 2 Timothy 3:16–17.

If the preacher is dealing with non-narrative prose, he or she may list the truths that the text affirms and synthesize them with information obtained from the outline of the text. This will give him or her the major emphasis of the text. This emphasis is the major subject or topic of the text that may be used in deriving the theme of the text.

The literary interpretation as a whole is synthesized with the "Sharpening The Sword –Section IV." When this is accomplished, we have a handle on what the text means. We must now ask ourselves, "How does this text function in the context of the Bible book?" In order to answer this question, we must merge the literary interpretation with the historical interpretation "in seeking to understand the message of the text in its own historical setting." We can never underestimate the importance of the historical setting. The following poem by an unnamed Bible scholar, included in Palmer's book *How to Understand the Bible,* illustrates this fact.

Rules of Interpretation

It shall greatly help thee to understand Scripture

If thou mark

Not Only what is spoken or written

But of Whom And To Whom Wit

what words At

what time Where,

With what circumstances

Considering what goeth before And what followeth.

Historical interpretation has two main parts. First, we take the fruit of the grammatical and literary interpretations, i.e., the meaning of the message to us. Second, we must understand that meaning in the context of the passage's historical setting. Then, we can discover the author's intended meaning of the text and the needs of the author's intended audience.

In discovering the author's intended meaning of the text, we must understand that it will always be in harmony with the immediate, sectional, and book context because the text originated in the mind of God (2 Timothy 3:16–17 NKJV). The author's intended meaning will always conform to the environment of the author. The text was not written in a vacuum. As Palmer posits, "The author drew upon the customs of his day, the opinions of his time, the circumstances surrounding his life, and the nature of his own personality" (1980, page number). This is commonly referred to as the life situation or setting of the author and his audience. In determining the author's intended meaning for the original hearers/recipients, we ask the following questions: Who is speaking or writing the message? To whom is the message addressed? When was this message spoken? Where was the message spoken? About whom was this message spoken? Why was the message spoken? What were the circumstances?

Understanding the life situation behind the text provides valuable insight into understanding the purpose of the writing. Bryson proposes that "the interpreter's task is to probe for the original purpose of the passage" (1995, page number). This technique guards against perverting the author's purpose of the passage and ensures that the preacher is cutting it straight during the exegesis. We seek to impress the author's intended meaning of the text upon the contemporary listener.

The second question under historical interpretation is which of the audience's needs the author sought to address. Was it faithfulness, disobedience, idolatry, injustice, half-heartedness, or rebellion against God? Every text is written with a purpose in mind (2 Timothy 3:6–17 NKJV). When we look at the message of the text in light of the life situation and the audience's need, we gain a vivid understanding of the author's original message. We now must take and examine the text from a theocentric point of view.

Theocentric interpretation involves questioning what the passage reveals about God, His redemptive acts, His covenants, His grace, and His will for His people. We know that God is always the main attraction and that humans are mere players on life's stage. Theocentric interpretation ensures that God receives all the glory and that humans are not glorified through moralizations of the Biblical text. If done properly, theocentric interpretation will build a hedge around our tendencies to preach moral stories instead of the all-wise counsel of God.

Theocentric interpretation can also provide links to Christian preaching from the Old Testament. Jesus Christ proclaimed in John

10:30 (KJV), "'I and the Father are one.'" Even though this may be proof-texting to many, if you can find God in the Old Testament, you will find Jesus in the New Testament doing the Father's will in a harmonizing way.

In light of God's will for His people, we now have an understanding of the author's intended message for the people of God. We now must continue cutting it straight by summarizing the textual theme and textual purpose.

Wisdom is the principal thing; therefore get wisdom:
and with all thy getting get understanding.

—PROVERBS 4:7 (KJV)

Chapter 6

CUTTING IT STRAIGHT BY UNDERSTANDING THE WHAT AND THE WHY OF THE TEXT

Wisdom is the principal thing; therefore get wisdom:
and with all thy getting get understanding.

—PROVERBS 4:7 (KJV)

In all the "getting" that we have done thus far, if we don't get an understanding of the textual theme and textual purpose, then our "getting" is in vain.

We discovered the subject or focus during the combining of our "Sharpening the Sword" (Part III) and the literary interpretation (Part IV). In order to preach an expository sermon, we need more than the singular subject or composite truth that the text projects. We must develop a summary sentence of the subject or the composite truth that the text asserts. In other words, we must describe *what* the author is saying about the subject or composite truth of the text. The textual theme answers the question, "What is the author's point for the original hearers?" The textual theme should be formulated as an assertion with a subject (composite truth) and a predicate (verb phrase). Many expositors have suggested the sentence be stated in past tense to function in the sermon theme as a summary sentence in present tense. The sermon theme may sometimes be synonymous with the textual theme. In order to preach the "whole counsel of God," the author's point for the original audience must be the same for the contemporary audience in the light of the New Testament and the New Covenant.

The purpose of the passage may be to persuade, to admonish, to warn, to inform, to encourage, or to rebuke. However, the preacher needs to write a specific summary sentence of the purpose or goal of the text. The textual purpose of the passage answers the questions "Why was the selected passage written?" and "What specific needs/problems of the recipients/readers does the passage address?"

The specific textual goal sentence is the first step towards establishing relevance of the sermon to the contemporary hearer. Greidanus states that "This insight transports preachers halfway to conceiving a relevant sermon. The other half is discovering the same or similar need among the contemporary hearers" (1999 or 1988, page number).

Now that we have an understanding of the message of the text, have capsulated that message into a theme sentence, and have a sentence stating the specific textual/author's goal, we now will continue cutting it straight by rightly dividing the canon and the covenants.

> But the word of the LORD was unto them precept
> upon precept, precept upon precept; line upon line,
> line upon line; here a little, and there a little.

—ISAIAH 28:13 (KVJ)

Chapter 7

CUTTING IT STRAIGHT BY RIGHTLY DIVIDING THE CANON AND THE COVENANT

But the word of the LORD was unto them precept
upon precept, precept upon precept; line upon line,
line upon line; here a little, and there a little.

—ISAIAH 28:13 (KVJ)

*U*nder this section, we seek to determine two facts. Does our discovered message of the text harmonize with the sixty-six books of the Bible? Is the message relevant in the light of the New Testament covenant? The answers to these questions will determine if our discovered message is scriptural or un-scriptural and if we have the linkage and basis for the Christian proclamation of the discovered message in the Old Testament.

Palmer writes that "the 66 books of the Bible are separate, yet not disconnected fragments. Truth is a harmonious whole and these separate works all blend into one grand work" (1980, page number). Someone once said, "The Bible is the mind of God." One Spirit inspired some forty different writers over a space of 1500 years to write the Bible (2 Peter 1:19–21 NKJV). This fact infers that the textual theme and the discovered message of the text must be in total harmony with the canon.

Palmer presents *five harmonies* that exist within the sixty-six books of the Bible. They are as follows.

> The harmony of *purpose*: God revealing his will to sinful men in order for him to be saved or redeemed; the harmony of *theme*: The history, the nature, and the hope of this grand theme of redemption is the very thing that unites all these separate books into one Bible...this theme shapes the design of each book no matter what style or method its author used; the harmony of *story*: The coming of Christ is the real story of the whole Bible; the harmony of *structure*: Each book is essential to the Bible as a whole. Each has a function in the total book; the harmony of *doctrine*: There is one harmonious flow of teaching throughout the Bible. (198, page number; emphasis added)

Our interpretation, i.e., a broken line in the harmony of the whole Bible, must be in harmony with all sixty-six books. Therefore, the textual theme assertion and textual purpose must be in harmony with these five harmonies in order to be the rightly divided Word of God. If this is not the case, we should again review "Cutting It Straight by Rightly Dividing the Interpretations" (Part IV).

The second question we ask is this: "Is the message of the text relevant in light of the New Testament Covenant?" The examination of the message in this light will determine if we have a linkage and basis to preach a Christian message from the Old Testament text.

Most theologians will agree with the idea that the Bible is a progressive revelation and that the story of the Bible unfolds or is progressively revealed to man. As W. Robert Palmer suggests, "The Bible unfolds according to the personal relationship between God, the author, and man the reader" (1980, page number). God entered into these relationships via covenants. A covenant, in its most simple form, is an agreement or contract entered into by two parties "binding them together to do things on behalf of each other." If we examine the canon, we can see the progressiveness of the covenants in the whole Bible. There are covenants made with individuals, such as Noah, before and after the flood, and with Abraham and David. There is the covenant of law made with Israel as a nation. Finally, there is the New Testament covenant of grace made with the human family through faith in Christ Jesus.

The terms, some promises, some prohibitions, some commands are specific in each covenant. Warnings, examples, and the eternal truth principles pertaining to the nature and the character of God appear to be more transferable between the Old and New Testament covenants. If our discovered textual theme and purpose is in harmony with the canon and the New Testament Covenant, we turn our attention to determining the relevance of the textual theme and its purpose in light of the New Testament Covenant and contemporary culture.

> For whatever things were written before were written
> for our learning, that we through the patience and
> comfort of the Scriptures might have hope.
>
> **—ROMANS 15:4 (NKJV)**

Chapter 8

CUTTING IT STRAIGHT BY RIGHTLY DETERMINING THE RELEVANCE OF THE MESSAGE IN LIGHT OF THE NEW TESTAMENT AND THE CONTEMPORARY CULTURE

For whatever things were written before were written
for our learning, that we through the patience and
comfort of the Scriptures might have hope.

—ROMANS 15:4 (NKJV)

The message discovered in our selected text must be examined for relevance under the light of the New Testament Covenant and in the context of contemporary culture. Osborne suggests that before we can contextualize the passage, "we must determine the extent to which it is meant for our day" (1991, page number). I believe that for any message to be a Christian message, it must be able to be contextualized and applied to the modern day hearer in harmony with the New Testament Covenant and the contemporary culture. As Christian preachers, we must ask ourselves if the teaching/message of the passage is valid in light of the New Testament Covenant. Is the teaching/message applicable in the contemporary culture? If the answers to these two questions are yes, then the message has the greatest opportunity to be preached as a unique Christian message.

Theological truths, such as God is gracious, and moral truths, such as the prohibition against adultery, are valid teachings under the Old Testament Covenant as well as the New Testament Covenant. Theological truths and moral truths usually can be preached as Christian.

The New Covenant serves as a divine limit that helps filter out Old Testament messages and precepts that are not uniquely Christian. Some preachers prefer to broaden their bases for Christian messages to include all of the New Testament. I disagree with that concept because some of the New Testament narratives are clearly presented in the context of the Old Testament Covenant and may cause some preachers to preach a fifth gospel. All scripture is inspired but no preachers are inspired (2 Timothy 3:16–17 NKJV). If the preacher follows after Paul as he followed after Christ (1 Corinthians 11:1 NKJV), then he is assured of a Christian message. We, as Christian preachers, must stay true to biblical patterns. If we follow the New Testament apostles' examples, methodologies, and their applications of theological and moral truths, then we are assured of proclaiming a relevant Christian message. Paul writes to Timothy in 2 Timothy 1:13 (NKJV), informing him, "Hold fast the pattern of sound words which you have heard from me, in faith and love which are in Christ Jesus." Let us continue cutting it straight by determining the relevancy of the message in light of the New Covenant.

Is the message relevant in the context of contemporary culture? This is important to know, as the purpose and behavior that God desires must be applicable. Usually, the New Covenant will filter out most of the problems in making an application for contemporary hearers. If the preacher stays with the theological and moral truths that are not culturally sensitive, then he or she should be able to proclaim a uniquely Christian message.

Now that we have determined the relevancy of the message for Christian preaching, let us continue cutting it straight as we move to sermon development.

So they read in the book in the law of God
distinctly, and gave the sense, and caused
them to understand the reading.

—NEHEMIAH 8:8 (KJV)

PART IV

DEVELOPING THE MESSAGE

Chapter 9

CUTTING IT STRAIGHT WHEN DEVELOPING THE SERMON/ BIBLICAL PRESENTATION

So they read in the book in the law of God
distinctly, and gave the sense, and caused
them to understand the reading.

—NEHEMIAH 8:8 (KJV)

A sermon may simply be defined as an exposition, illustration, and application of what the eternal truth of the Biblical text means to the hearer in our contemporary world. Since each Biblical text contains the elements of time, distance, and culture, the sermon must effectively overcome these barriers and cause the hearers of today to "understand the meaning" (Nehemiah 8:8 NIV). In order to continue cutting it straight when developing the sermon, there are six steps that I suggest the preacher take to reach this goal.

Step 1: Decide on a sermon *theme*

Step 2: Select a *title* for the sermon

Step 3: Decide on the *purpose* of the sermon

Step 4: Decide *how the message can be proclaimed* as a Christian message

Step 5: Decide on the *design* of the sermon

Step 6: *Implement* the sermon

Step 1 is to decide on the sermon theme. If you have been following this guide, you should now have an idea of the textual theme in your mind. The sermon theme, in order to be a biblical sermon and a uniquely Christian message, must be founded upon the textual theme. The sermon theme is a precise summary sentence of what the sermon will address in the present tense. The sermon theme focuses the sermon on a particular idea, not multiple ideas. If someone comments that your sermon had "many good points," it can be an indication that your sermon lacked focus. A short cut for a sermon theme is to state *the textual theme in the present tense.* This is a simple method to use and will provide the basis for a biblical message.

Step 2 is selecting a title for the sermon. The title of the sermon should capsulate the essence of what the sermon is about and should be easy to remember. I try to title the sermon in so it serves as a memory peg that relates to the proposition or God's solution in the sermon. For example, my sermon on Matthew 22:1–14 (KJV), "The Parable of Wedding Banquet," I titled "All Dressed up with No Place to Go." The sermon demonstrated the futility of being justified by the clothes of our own self-righteousness (our works). People still remember that message over ten years after I preached it because of the title. Now that we have the title of the sermon in hand, let us decide on the purpose of the sermon.

Step 3 is to decide on the purpose of the sermon based upon the textual purpose. It literally answers the question "What is the response that God desires of the people who first heard or received the message of the text?" Just as the sermon theme was based on the textual theme, in order to have a biblical purpose that is pleasing to God, the preacher must base the sermon's purpose on the original author's purpose, the inspired purpose of God. The apostle Peter writes in 2 Peter 2:19 (KJV) that the apostles have a "more sure word of prophecy" that supercedes an eyewitness account and surely any invention of our minds, "knowing this first, that no Scripture is on any private interpretation" (2 Peter 1:19 KJV). Asking what response the inspired writer sought from his audience, and answering this question based on the text, we are able to discern the inspired author's intended purpose in *a general sense*. For the purpose to be of benefit in our message, we must write *a concise statement* about the general purpose in a *specific sense*. Bryson refers to this concise statement as the "sermon objective sentence." The sermon purpose sentence is *a concise sentence* of what the sermon is asking God's people to do. I would like to suggest that the appeal for this action be done with a view toward the love, grace, and tender mercies of God. This will help keep from exalting human beings. In Romans 12:1–2 (KJV), Paul's purpose, that the believer's action be transformed, is with a view toward the tender mercies of God.

The purpose of the sermon should be stated in a way that reveals the desire of the preacher and the desired response of the hearers. However, remember that the preacher's desired response must be in harmony with the desired response intended by God through the inspired author. The sermon purpose sentence is a declarative sentence that expresses what the preacher wants the people to do upon hearing the sermon.

It is a good idea to write the sermon purpose sentence on a three inch by five inch index card and keep the purpose of the sermon before you as you develop the sermon. The sermon purpose sentence could be stated as follows for Romans 12:1–2 (KJV): In view of God's tender mercies, I want to inspire the congregation to live transformed lives. The sermon purpose sentence will help give your sermon focus and filter out unrelated information. Now that we have *the sermon theme, the sermon title,* and *the sermon purpose,* we can decide how they can be used to preach a uniquely Christian message.

Step 4 is deciding on how the sermon theme and sermon purpose may be preached as a Christian message.

> For whatsoever things were written aforetime were written for our learning, that we through patience and comfort of the scriptures might have hope. (Romans 15:4 KJV)

> Hold fast the form of sound words, which thou hast heard of me, in faith and love which is in Christ Jesus. (2 Timothy 1:13 KJV)

Many preachers have invented allegories out of delusion to impose a teaching or purpose based on their personal theologies and prejudices without being aware. In Jesus Christ's prayer for his disciples in John 17:6–19 (KJV), the Lord tells His disciples to sanctify (*hagaizo*) or set themselves apart for sacred use by the "truth [because] your word is truth." This imperative is given to the disciples who would become Christ's apostles. From this, we infer that future believers would be sanctified by the apostolic truth or teaching. Notice in Acts 2:42 (KJV) that Luke writes as a historian, saying that the early church "devoted themselves to the apostles' teaching and fellowship." If this is the case (and it is), a Christian message must be in harmony not only with what Christ taught, but also in harmony with what the apostles taught. When using an Old Testament textual theme and purpose as the foundation for a Christian message, this textual theme and purpose must be in harmony with what the Lord Jesus Christ taught and what apostles taught.

Notice Paul's teaching on marriage in 1 Corinthians 7:10 (NKJV): "Now to the married I command, yet not I but the Lord: a wife is not to depart from her husband." Paul seems to make sure that he does not introduce a new commandment or teaching on the subject of divorce. In 1 Corinthians 7:25 (NKJV), Paul writes: "Now concerning virgins: I have no commandment from the Lord; yet I give judgment as one whom the Lord in his mercy has made trustworthy." How was Paul made "trustworthy"? 1 Timothy1:11(NKJV) gives valuable insight into the things that made Paul "trustworthy" to have an opinion unsupported by direct inference or quotation or teaching. The apostle writes that he "was appointed a preacher, *an apostle*, and a teacher of the Gentiles" (emphasis added). I believe what made Paul completely trustworthy was that Paul was an apostle inspired by the Holy Spirit. We preachers of today are not "inspired"; therefore, in order to cut it straight, we must harmonize the Old Testament theme and purpose with the teaching of Christ and the apostles to have a uniquely Christian message. Many times, a preacher may have the theme and purpose of the Old Testament passage correct. However, if it does not harmonize with the teaching of Christ and the apostles in theme, purpose, and application, the preacher can proclaim a fifth gospel that is in error. In order to have a "trustworthy" message, we must defer to the apostolic themes, purpose, and application to ensure that we have unique Christian preaching. Paul writes in 1 Corinthians 11:1 (KJV) that we should be followers of him as he is of Christ. We must hold to the apostolic pattern to continue cutting it straight. Below are some examples of connecting the Old Testament to the New Testament using "trustworthy" methods.

- Old Testament scripture cited by Christ and affirmed by apostolic teaching:

    o Jesus Christ/Genesis 2:26 (KJV)
    o Paul/1 Corinthians 7 (KJV)

- Old Testament prophesy cited by Jesus Christ or apostle:

    o Jesus Christ/Luke 4:18–19 and 21 (KJV)
    o Peter/Acts 2:17–21 (KJV)

- Old Testament scripture cited as an allegory:

    o Apostle Paul/Galatians 3:21–25 (NKV)

- Old Testament typology cited by Jesus Christ or apostle:

    o Jesus Christ/Matthew 12:40 (KJV)
    o 1 Peter 3:20–21 (KJV)

- Old Testament scripture directly quoted by Christ or apostle that is affirmed by apostolic application/teaching:

    It is good to verify the application/teaching of Old Testament passages with the apostle's application/teaching to ensure that the message of the sermon will be a uniquely Christian message. We are able to rely on the apostles' teachings and applications because they were, and are, the only competent administrators of the New Testament covenant.

  o The apostle Paul writes in 2 Corinthians 3:5–6 (NIV), "Not that we are competent in ourselves to claim anything for ourselves, but our competence comes from God. *He has made us competent as ministers of a new covenant* not of the letter but of the Spirit; for the letter kills, but the Spirit gives life" (emphasis added).

In making the connection to the New Testament, the preacher's message must be in harmony with the apostolic teachings. Preachers must not go beyond what is written. Paul exhorts preachers to this standard in 1 Corinthians 4:6 (NIV).

    Now, brothers, I have applied these things to myself and Apollos for your benefit, so that you may learn from us the meaning of the saying, "Do not go beyond what is written." Then you will not take pride in one man over against another.

In order to have an opportunity to proclaim a uniquely Christian message, we must continue cutting it straight by not going beyond what is a written and clearly definable or inferable apostolic application. Now that we verified that we have a New Testament connection that it harmonizes with apostolic teachings and applications, we can decide on the design of the sermon.

Step 5 is designing the sermon. The sermon design is the structure of rhetorical form the preacher selects to proclaim God's word. The structure of a sermon is the package in which the content (God's will and purpose) of the sermon resides. No matter how good a product may be, the type of packaging can aid in the delivery and purchase of the product.

Bryson writes that structuring a sermon may be compared to packaging a product for sale: "the contents have more importance then the packaging, but the container helps purchasers buy and transport the product" (1995, page number). If we want people to effectively hear what God is saying to them and retain it, we must pay close attention to sermon design. In deciding a sermon design, the literary form of the selected preaching text provides a valuable clue on how to proceed, and it can serve as a basis our final sermon design. We all agree that the inspired author who wrote the text has, by far, the best form. *The best approach is to pattern our sermon form after the inspired author whenever possible.*

Expository preaching in a classical sense obtains its main point and supporting points from the selected text. Traditionally, the deductive design and the inductive design have been the mainstays of twentieth-century preaching forms.

The deductive sermon design uses a general main point that is supported by specific sub-points and is usually structured as illustrated below.

I.   General main point

   A. Deductive supportive sub-point
   B. Deductive supported sub-point

II. General main point

   A. Deductive supportive sub-point
   B. Deductive supported sub-point

The inductive sermon design reasons from the supportive sub-points to the main point and is usually structured as illustrated below.

A. Deductive supportive sub-point

B. Deductive supportive sub-point

   I. Main point

A. Deductive supportive sub-point

A. Deductive supportive sub-point

   I. Main point

These sermon designs are usually sufficient for most sermons. However, the diverse nature of the Old Testament writings requires that the preacher investigate and study many sermon designs. Not only does the genre of the passage impact sermon design, but the preacher must take into account the audience who will hear the sermon. A sermon is proclaimed, but is it heard? Faith comes by hearing by the Word of God (Romans 10:17 KJV). Bryson suggests that "the choice of structural designs most depends on the nature of the audience, the personality of the preacher, and the shape of the text" (1995, 344). If the preacher neglects to take the nature of the audience and his or her personality into consideration, he or she may preach the word but never be heard.

The sermon must not be designed in a vacuum. The twenty-first century presents a great challenge for preachers who expound the gospel. Contemporary listeners are accustomed to multiple forms of communication. Many homileticians of today believe that the *lecture type* of sermon can no longer be the only sermon design used by the preacher. We live in an age where people no longer want to hear a lecture. It is almost as if they must see the sermon. I believe that we have seen the last days of three points and a poem. The following sermon design is adapted from a guideline presented by Elbert E. Elliot of the Trinity Theological College and Seminary during his seminar "Preaching to the Mass Media Generation."

This is a form that, I believe, adapts to the Hebrew narratives of the Old Testament and creates and maintains interest in the sermon for the twenty-first-century listener. I have used this design as a guide and have had success. I call it the A Plus sermon design; that stands for *attraction*, *argument*, and *appeal*. These terms correspond to the traditional introduction, body, and conclusion. I use these terms because it provides me with a focused idea of what each section of the sermon design must accomplish to be effective. I start each section with the goal of that section in mind. A general outline of this sermon design is as follows.

A) The Attraction

1. Create an interest based on an unmet contemporary human dilemma/need synonymous with the human dilemma/ need resident in the selected text. We must get the listener

to leave the door of his or her mind cracked open. If we show up on the listener's doorstep with something he or she can do without, we receive a "thanks, but no thanks," and the door closes on the sermon. Make the need real for the contemporary listeners.

2. Connect to the listener by relating three relevant affirmations about the contemporary need. Use relevant illustrations, parallelisms of facts, or relative questions pertaining to the unmet contemporary need that will evoke a "yes" response in the mind of your listeners. Try to get the listeners into a positive mindset about the sermon that is about to come. We want the listener to feel that the information is vital, and so open the door of his or her mind. If the preacher is successful, the door of the listener's mind opens, the preacher is invited in, and the preacher has made the connection with the listener.

Transition:

3. Direct the listener to the selected text and read the Word of God distinctively.

4. Transition to the argument section of the sermon by introducing the discussion of the unmet human need/ contemporary need found in the text.

B) The Argument

The purpose of the argument is to present evidence that will demand a verdict in the appeal section of this sermon design:

1. Show evidence of the unmet human need/contemporary human need exemplified by the text.

2. Show evidence of the unmet human need/contemporary need satisfied by God's grace and truth from the biblical text. Remember that God's grace and truth may also come through chosen human vessels by His providence.

3. Show evidence of the unmet human need/contemporary human need in light of the Christ (grace and truth), the apostle's doctrine, and the New Covenant.

C) The Appeal

1. Picture the purpose: Picture what the listener must do! Use the sermon purpose that you wrote on the index card at the beginning of sermon preparation.

2. Picture the spiritual and emotional satisfaction that results when one obeys God's solution in the light of Christ (grace and truth), the apostle's doctrine, and the New Covenant. (Use predictive statements such as "When one repents..."

(predictive outcome). Predictive statements help develop a sense of expectation for the listener.

3. Picture the spiritual and emotional consequences that result when one rejects God's solution in the light of Christ (grace and truth), the apostle's doctrine, and the New Covenant.

4. Incredible emotional appeal to accept God's grace and truth in love. (Speak from the heart).

5. Offer the listener Christ.

Step 6 is the implementation of the sermon design. There is nothing new for implementing the sermon. Most all homileticians suggest that we start *first* with the appeal or conclusion. The appeal focuses on the purpose and the desired response that God wants from His people. We must implement the sermon with a destination in mind. By doing this, we help the sermon to be focused. The appeal/conclusion is designed with the purpose of the sermon as the focal point. The index note card with the purpose clearly written on it should be in front of us while we write our appeal/conclusion.

The appeal must picture the emotional and spiritual satisfaction that one will receive if one appropriates God's solution for his or her life as well as the consequences of rejecting God's solution. Contrasting the benefits and consequences of accepting or rejecting God's solution must develop a powerful picture in order for the hearer to make a decision. The use of predictive statements in presenting

God's solution using *when* and *then* may be paired together. An example is "When one obeys the gospel of Christ, then he or she is saved."

The attraction/introduction must attract the listener's attention by creating a reason to hear the rest of the sermon. The attraction/introduction must build a bridge for the listener to the first point, move, or concept in the sermon argument.

The sermon argument/body of the sermon is the last design implemented. The argument/body presents the human dilemma and God's solution whatever to whatever that dilemma may be. The argument/body of the sermon is composed of elements that support the sermon theme/proposition based on exposition of the selected text.

The argument may consist of the sermon design that is most suitable for the gospel message to be communicated without perversion of the intended meaning of the text. Usually, the literary form of the argument is in harmony and is complementary to the inspired literary form of the selected text.

Step 6 involves writing the sermon out in the oral cultural language of the hearer. As preachers, we must remember that the Bible is written to be heard and remembered. Therefore, sermons must be expounded to be heard and remembered. Faith comes by hearing and hearing by the Word of God.

Paul sought to be all things to all people for the gospel's sake. Let our sermons be likewise. Let them be preached in such a manner that God's word of grace is communicated so people may hear the Word and remember the Word. Writing the sermon out in oral form is helpful not only for those who hear us, but it is also helpful for us.

Writing the sermon out in oral form helps the preacher internalize the ideas of the sermon that he or she wants to communicate. The writing of the sermon is not for memorization but to help us clarify our ideas. Dale Carnegie suggests that if our "ideas are clear then the words will come naturally and unconsciously" (1992, page number). Now let us continue cutting it straight when delivering the sermon.

Take heed to yourself and to the doctrine.
Continue in them, for in doing this you will save
both yourself and those who hear you.

—1 TIMOTHY 4:16 (NKJV)

PART V

DELIVERING THE SERMON/BIBLICAL PRESENTATION

Chapter 10

CUTTING IT STRAIGHT BY PREPARING TO SOUND YOUR TRUMPET

Take heed to yourself and to the doctrine.
Continue in them, for in doing this you will save
both yourself and those who hear you.

—1 TIMOTHY 4:16 (NKJV)

In order to preach the word and "be instant in season and out of season" (2 Timothy 4:2 NKJV), the preacher must be prepared to preach the word utilizing personal preparation and delivery preparation to be pulpit ready. In other words, the preacher must be ready to lift up his or her voice like a trumpet. At least three aspects of personal preparation are critical to the preacher's personal preparation: prayer, passion, and power.

The preacher must continually stay in prayer in order to stay focused on his or her task and the leading of the Holy Spirit. If the preacher is to be spiritually minded, he or she must set his or her mind on spiritual things through prayer by "praying consistently" (1 Thessalonians 5:17 NKJV) and living out his or her daily life according to the Spirit (Romans 8:4 KJV). When the preacher is focused on spiritual things through prayer, he or she will be spiritually minded.

Secondly, the preacher must maintain a passion for preaching the Word. The preacher's zeal must be greater than his or her personal pride and ego. The passion for the preached Word must consume him or her. Listen to Jeremiah, who writes, "Then I said, I will not make mention of him, nor speak any more in his name. But his word was in mine heart as a burning fire shut up in my bones, and I was weary with forbearing, and I could not stay" (Jeremiah 20:9 KJV).

Our passion for preaching must consume us because of the great love demonstrated by the Lord Jesus Christ's death for us. While we were yet still sinners held captive by our selfish lusts and blinded by sin, the Lord Jesus Christ died for us (Romans 5:8 KJV). We must always remember our great indebtedness to the Lord Jesus Christ. Someone put it this way: "The Lord Jesus Christ paid a debt He did not owe for humanity who could not pay." Paul expressed this sense of indebtedness in Romans 1:14–16 (KJV): "I am debtor both to the Greeks, and to the Barbarians; both to the wise, and to the unwise.

So, as much as in me is, I am ready to preach the gospel to you that are at Rome also. For I am not ashamed of the gospel of Christ: for it is the power of God unto salvation to every one that believeth to the Jew first, but also to the Greek."

We as preachers must maintain this sense of indebtedness to help preserve our passion. Where would we be if someone had not shared the glorious gospel of the Lord Jesus Christ with us? The preacher not only prepares himself or herself through prayer, and by preserving his or her passion with a sense of love for the Lord and indebtedness to others. He or she also must have power.

The power to preach the Word is not dependent solely on the power in the voice but also of the Holy Spirit. When the preacher continues in prayer throughout the preaching preparation, he or she is able to preach the Word in season and out of season with power assisted by the Holy Spirit. The apostle Paul, writing in 1 Thessalonians 1:5 (KJV), says: "For our gospel came not unto you in word only, but also in power, and in the Holy Ghost, and in much assurance; as ye know what manner of men we were among you for your sake." In Ephesians 3:14–19 (KJV), Paul writes these words concerning the power available to strengthen the "inner man."

> That he would grant you, according to the riches of
> his glory, to *be strengthened with might by his Spirit*

in the inner man; That Christ may dwell in your hearts by faith; that ye, being rooted and grounded in love, May be able to comprehend with all saints what is the breadth, and length, and depth, and height; And to know the love of Christ, which passeth knowledge, that ye might be filled with all the fulness of God. Now unto him that is able to do exceeding abundantly above all that we ask or think, *according to the power that worketh in us.* (Eph 3:16–20 KJV; emphasis added)

Our personal preparation is not only for the gospel's sake; it is also for our hearers' sakes. Notice again as the apostle Paul warns the young preacher Timothy in 1 Timothy 4:12–16 (NKJV).

Let no one despise your youth, but be an example to the believers in word, in conduct, in love, in spirit, in faith, in purity, Till I come, give attention to reading, to exhortation, to doctrine. Do not neglect the gift that is in you, which was given to you by prophecy with the laying on of the hands of the eldership. Meditate on these things; give yourself entirely to them, that your progress may be evident to all. Take heed to yourself and to the doctrine. Continue in them, for in doing this you will save both yourself and those who hear you.

Let us be personally prepared to *preach the word!*

> Cry aloud, spare not, lift up thy voice like a
> trumpet, and shew my people their transgression,
> and the house of Jacob their sins.

—ISAIAH 58:1 (KJV)

Chapter 11

CUTTING IT STRAIGHT WHEN SOUNDING YOUR TRUMPET

Cry aloud, spare not, lift up thy voice like a
trumpet, and shew my people their transgression,
and the house of Jacob their sins.

—ISAIAH 58:1 (KJV)

I charge thee therefore before God, and the Lord
Jesus Christ, who shall judge the quick and the
dead at his appearing and his kingdom; Preach the
word; be instant in season, out of season; reprove,
rebuke, exhort with all longsuffering and doctrine.

—2 TIMOTHY 4:1–2 (KJV)

*W*hen our personal preparation is set, then we must prepare to preach the Word. Delivery of the message entails final preparations that will continue to develop the preacher's confidence in his or her ability to preach the Word with courage and confidence. I suggest that in his or her final preparations, the preacher read the manuscript, reflect on the argument, review the illustrations, and recite the flow of the sermon.

The reading of the manuscript (expanded outline) continues to internalize the message. The goal of reading the manuscript is to internalize but not memorize the message. Any memorization of the message will take away from the spontaneity of the sermon. Someone once said that "a sermon is preached to be heard and not read." We as preachers want to preach from an overflow of knowledge about the sermon material and from familiarity with the contents. In this way, we are able to adjust the communication of the sermon to gain and maintain the listener's attention during the proclamation of the message. We want to own the message that we preach. God's message must be the preacher's message. If God's message fails to indwell the preacher (become part of the preacher), the message may sound like a reading of a third party's speech. Reading the manuscript is our last opportunity to indwell the message from God that we deliver. The apostle Peter writes, "If any man speak, let him speak as the oracles of God; if any man minister, let him do it as of the ability which God giveth: that God in all things may be glorified through Jesus Christ, to whom be praise and dominion for ever and ever. Amen" (1 Peter 4:11 KJV).

Let us read our manuscripts to help insure we are speaking the words of God. Not only must we read the manuscript, but we also must reflect on the purpose of the sermon that corresponds with the purpose of the inspired author of God. The idea of the sermon is to convey God's solution of the biblical text to people today. We must preach God's purpose and never lose sight of this goal. Paul warns the young preacher Timothy with these words: "Take heed unto thyself, and unto the doctrine; continue in them: for in doing this thou shalt both save thyself, and them that hear thee" (1 Timothy 4:16 KJV).

Someone once said, "Opinions are like noses: everybody has one." God's thoughts are not like our thoughts. Isaiah 55:7–9 (KVJ) informs us of this fact.

> Let the wicked forsake his way, and the unrighteous man his thoughts: and let him return unto the LORD, and he will have mercy upon him; and to our God, for he will abundantly pardon. For my thoughts are not your thoughts, neither are your ways my ways, saith the LORD. For as the heavens are higher than the earth, so are my ways higher than your ways, and my thoughts than your thoughts.

Let us preach the thoughts of God and not our own ideas that we may save ourselves and those who hear us.

After we have read the manuscript and reflected on the purpose, we must review the argument (points, moves, ideas) with the associated illustrations. The intent of this is to create a natural link or transition from the argument used in the sermon presentations. The illustrations should amplify the argument. Illustrations may be used generously, but they should not distract from the Word of God. After all, the message of God is not for entertainment. Dale Carnegie states that "most all people love a story" (1992, page number). Good illustrations that complement the Word of God will convey the relevancy of the message and provide support for the sermon argument.

After the preacher has read the manuscript, reflected on the purpose, and reviewed the argument along with the associated illustrations, he or she is pulpit ready: ready to preach the Word. The preacher may then feel as ready as the apostle Paul, who writes in his letter to the Romans, "So, as much as in me is, I am ready to preach the gospel to you that are at Rome also. For I am not ashamed of the gospel of Christ: for it is the power of God unto salvation to every one that believeth; to the Jew first, and also to the Greek" (Romans 1:15–16 KJV).

Preacher, preach the word!

PART VI

GOOD NEWS
YOU CAN USE

Chapter 12

GETTING A JUMP START

$\mathcal{H}$ere are some ideas from this five-part manual that you may use for immediate improvement in your sermon preparation and delivery.

1) Stay Plugged In

One of the things that may happen to the busy preacher in preparing sermons is spiritual dullness. This spiritual dullness, or worldly attitude, is brought about because of the lack of prayer and devotion in his or her personal life. The preacher must set aside time for prayer and devotion on a daily basis. A good devotional commentary will provide the preacher with variety for his or her daily devotions. If the preacher spends time with God on a consistent basis, he or she will find himself or herself becoming more spiritually minded.

Being spiritually minded helps us to be in step with the Holy Spirit and more sensitive to the Word of God. The apostle Paul writes in Colossians 3:16 (KJV) that we must "Let the word of Christ dwell in [us] richly in all wisdom"; when the Word of God indwells us, we are able to live the Word. Therefore, we walk the talk not just talk the walk.

2) The Whole Nine Yards

Using a conservative exegetical commentary to select the scriptural unit or the preaching text may reduce the time used for selecting a complete scriptural unit. However, this method will be only as good as the exegetical commentary you select. Beware of theological bias by the author and do not use exegetical commentaries for exposition of the scriptural unit at this point in your research of the text.

3) What's This?

When interpreting the message, quickly identify the genre of the Old Testament Bible book that you have selected. Examine the Bible book to see if its genre is Hebrew narrative, prophetic, law, wisdom, or psalms. This quick overview may give immediate insight into the genre of the scriptural unit and aid in your interpretation of the scriptural unit.

4) Sounding Your Trumpet

Here are some helpful hints to improve your delivery:

a) Be yourself; it's not worth being anyone else! Don't be pretentious in mannerisms or voice. Be yourself. Your holiness should be lived not just acted and talked.

b) Interact with the audience by maintaining eye contact. This will give the audience the sense that you are speaking to them individually. You want to be up close and personal.

c) Speak from the heart and not from the head

d) Speak from a sincere heart. You must believe what you are saying if you want others to believe.

REFERENCES

Achtemeier, Elizabeth. (1989). *Preaching From the Old Testament.* Louisville, Kentucky: Westminster/John Knox Press.

Bryson, Harold T. (1995). *Expository Preaching: The Art of Preaching Through the Bible.* Nashville, Tennessee: Broadman & Holman Publishers.

Carnegie, Dale. (1992). *The Quick and Easy Way to Effective Speaking.* Garden City, New York: Dale Carnegie and Associates, Inc.

Chapell, Bryan. (1994). *Christ Centered Preaching: Redeeming the Expository Sermon.* Grand Rapids, Michigan: Baker Book House Company.

Greidanus, Sidney. (1988). *The Modern Preacher and the Ancient Text: Interpreting And Preaching Biblical Literature.* Grand Rapids, Michigan: William B. Eerdmans Publishing Co.

———. (1999). *Preaching Christ from the Old Testament.* Grand Rapids, Michigan: William B. Eerdmans Publishing Co.

Loscalzo, Craig A. (1995). *Evangelistic Preaching That Connects: Guidance in Shaping Fresh and Appealing Sermons.* Downers Grove, Illinois: Intervarsity Press.

MacArthur Jr., John. (1992). *Rediscovering Expository Preaching.* Dallas, Texas: Word Publishing.

Osborne, Grant R. (1991). *The Hermeneutical Spiral: A Comprehensive Introduction of Biblical Interpretation.* Downers Grove, Illinois: Intervarsity Press.

Palmer, W. Robert. (1980). *How to Understand the Bible: Study Course for Youth and Adults.* Joplin, Missouri: College Press Publishing Company.

Proctor, Samuel D. (1994). *The Certain Sound of the Trumpet: Crafting a Sermon of Authority.* Valley Forge, Pennsylvania: Judson Press.

Robinson, Haddon W. (1980). *Biblical Preaching: The Development and Delivery of Expository Messages.* Grand Rapids, Michigan: Baker Book House.

Rogers, Richard. (1998). *The History of the Church in Acts.* Lubbock, Texas: Sunset International Bible Institute Press.

Printed in the United States
by Baker & Taylor Publisher Services